Longman
Splash!
3

• Brian Abbs • Anne Worrall • Ann Ward •

1 A message on the computer

Kate Lewis and Sam Roberts are at school. They are using the computer.

Practise with your friends.

1 Identity cards

 Who's speaking? Listen and point.

Identity card
Professor Wallace (scientist)
age: 35
birthday: May 4th
from: Malaysia
hair: black
eyes: brown

Identity card
Joseph Alexander (explorer)
age: 27
birthday: January 10th
from: USA
hair: red
eyes: green

Identity card
Mr Freeman (teacher) 
age: 30
birthday: September 22nd
from: England
hair: brown
eyes: blue

 Talk about the identity cards with your friend.

What's his name?   When's her birthday?   Where's she from?

 Make identity cards for yourself and your friend.

2 Where do they come from?

A puzzle. Read and match.

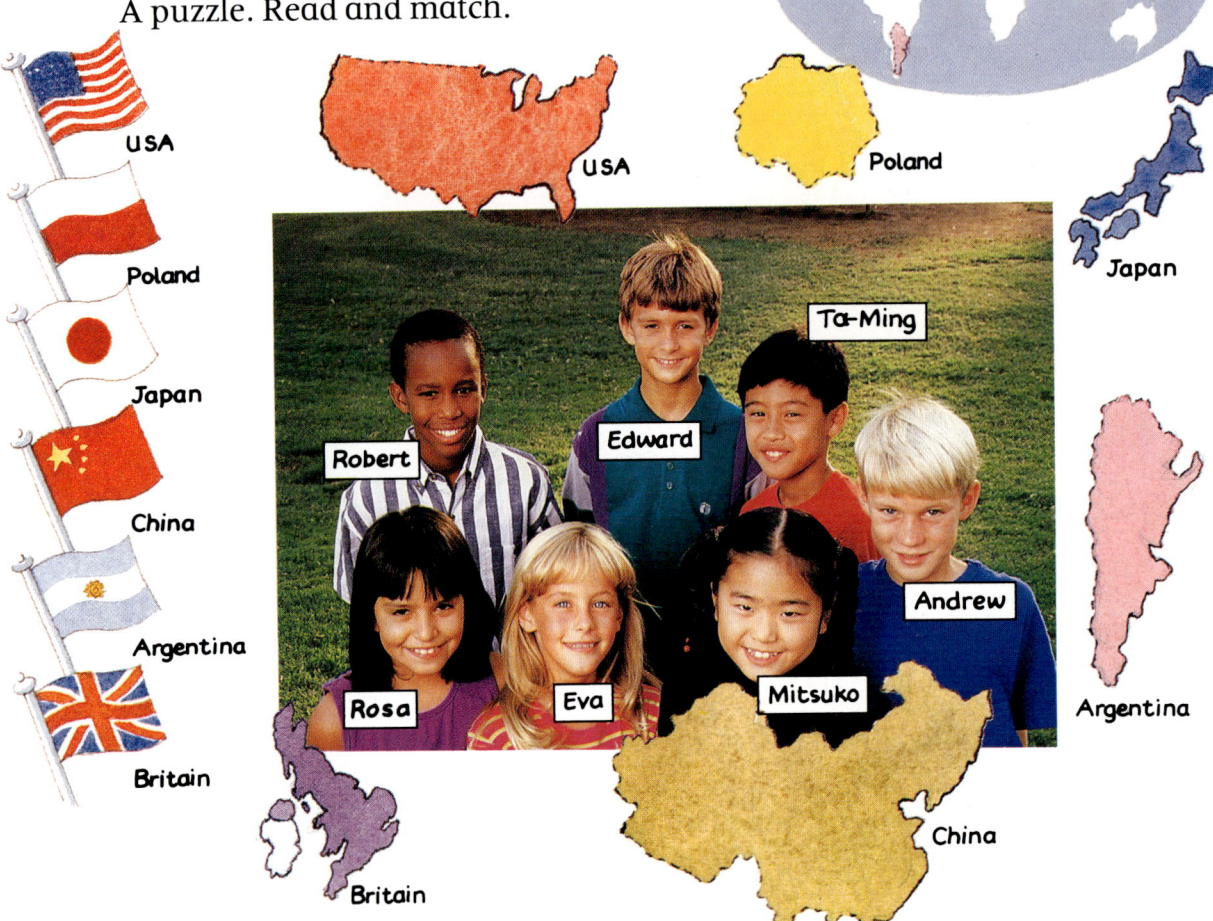

Robert comes from the USA. He's American.
Eva comes from Poland. She's Polish.
Mitsuko comes from Japan. She's Japanese.
Rosa comes from Argentina. She's Argentinian.
Ta-Ming comes from China. He's Chinese.
Andrew and Edward come from Britain. They're British.

Talk to your friend.

What nationality is Andrew? — *He's British.*

Where does Rosa come from? — *Argentina.*

Where do you come from? What's your nationality?

3 The Red Hand Gang

 Read and find.

WHERE ARE THE RED HAND GANG?

This is the Red Hand Gang. The leader of the gang is Mr Big. They call him 'The Boss'. Mr Big is very rich and lives on an island. He wants to own all the rare plants and animals in the world. Polly Zap is his assistant. At the moment she is in Indonesia in the rain forest. She is following Professor Wallace.
Zack is another member of the gang. He's short and he's got dark hair. He is in London now. Tex is in London, too. He's tall and he's got glasses. He's got a metal hand.

4 Who is it?

 Make questions about the Red Hand Gang. Ask your friend.

- They call him 'The Boss'. Who is it?
- Mr Big.
- She's got pink hair. Who is it?
- Polly Zap.

Remember!
What's ...?   She's got (pink hair)
Who ...?
Where ...?
When ...?

2 A computer magazine

🔴 This tiny microchip makes the computer work.

🔴 These children are learning to use a computer at school. They are using a keyboard and looking at the screen of the VDU*.

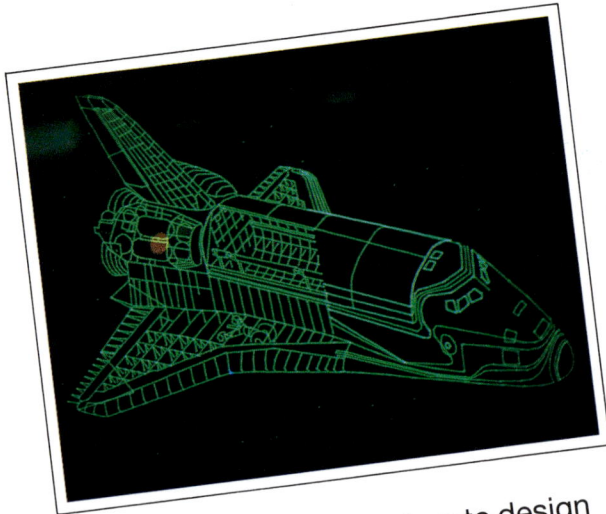

🔴 This woman works in an airport. She is finding seats on the plane for the passengers.

🔴 Engineers use computers to design things. This is the space shuttle.

* = Visual Display Unit

2

● The police use computers, too. Computers help them to find criminals. In this picture they are trying to identify a criminal.

● Computers are also fun! This boy is playing a computer game at home.

1 Who's speaking?

Listen to the conversations and point to the correct photo.

How many people in your class have got a computer? Ask your friends.

seven

2 What do they want to be?

Read and match.

I want to be an engineer.
I want to design planes.

We want to be pilots.
We want to fly planes.

I want to be a scientist.
I want to work in a laboratory.

I want to be a vet.
I want to look after sick animals.

I want to be a detective.
I want to catch criminals.

We want to be chefs. We want to cook wonderful food.

What do you want to be? Draw a picture and tell your friend.

I want to be an astronaut.   I want to go to the moon.

3 What do they do?

Listen to some people talking about their jobs and guess what they do.

A game. What do I do? Choose a job.
Your friend asks questions to guess what it is.

Do you use a computer?   Yes.

Are you a policeman?   No.

8
eight

4 Computer game

Tell Jack what to do.

| climb | cross | find | arrive | go | jump | run | swim |

1 ... the birthday cake in the shop.

2 ... up the ladder.

3 ... over the dog.

4 ... the road.

5 ... through the forest.

6 ... across the river.

7 ... away from the hungry cats.

8 ... at the party.

Remember!
What do you do?
What do you want to be?

3 In the rain forest

3

Oh, well. I've got my tent ... and lots of food and water.

I hope somebody has got my message!

 Practise with your friends.

1 Find the animals

Listen and point to the animals in the story.

 Talk to your friend.

Can you see a monkey? *Yes.*

How many monkeys are there? *There are three.*

2 True or false?

Listen and say.

The professor can use her computer ... *False.*

... but she can't climb down the cliff. *True.*

eleven

3 Where were they yesterday?

Read and match.

Carlo was at the video shop.
Steven was at home.
Simon was at the office.

Jane was at the newsagent's.
Sarah was at the station.
Alison was at the pizza parlour.

4 Who isn't telling the truth?

 Listen to an interview. One person isn't telling the truth. Who is it?

 Listen to Detective Casey's questions again. Practise them with your friend.

5 Talk to a detective

 Where were you last night? Think of a place and a time. Ask questions to find out where your friend was.

- Were you in the park last night?
- No, I wasn't.
- Were you in the video shop?
- Yes.

twelve

3

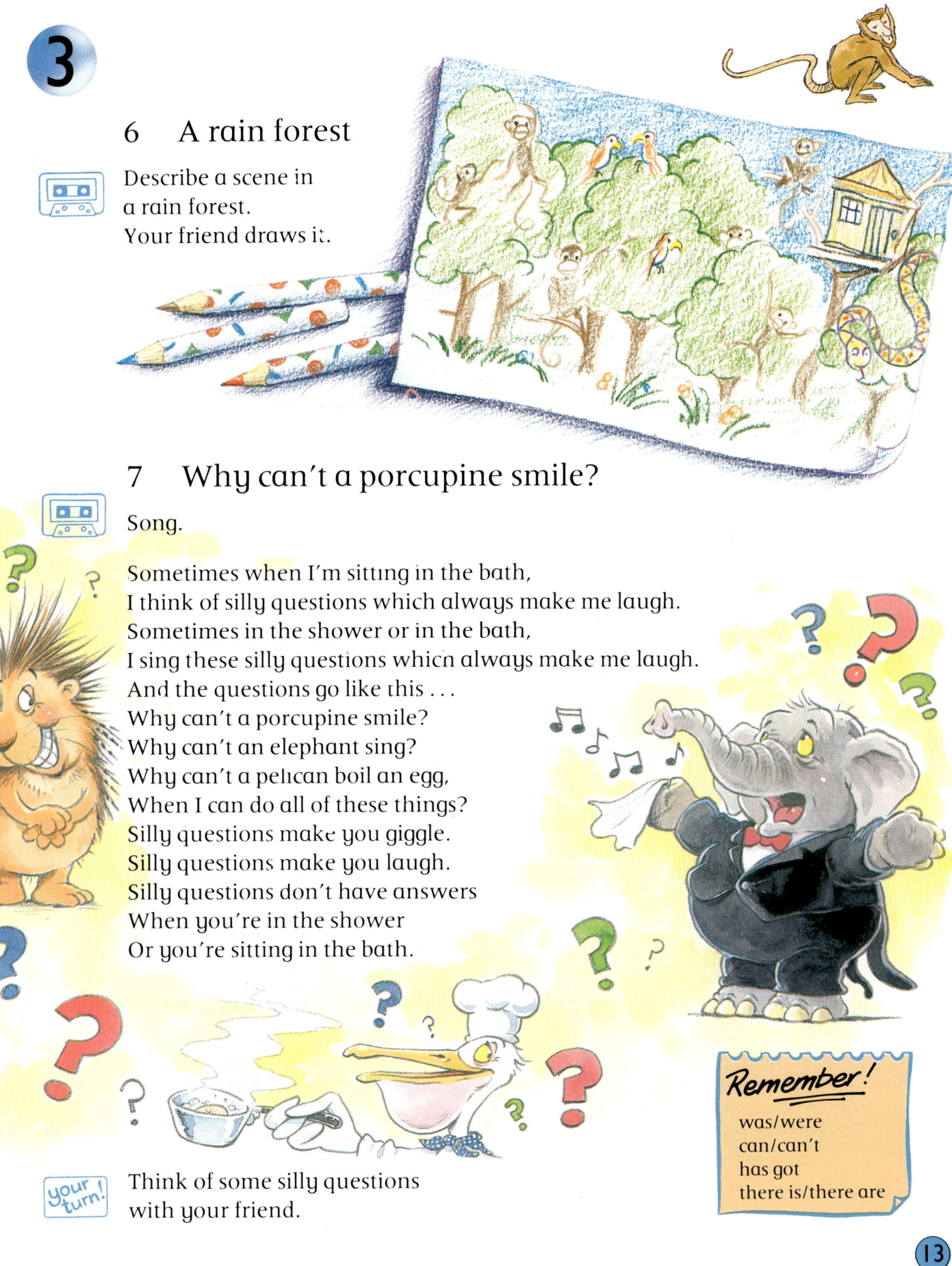

6 A rain forest

Describe a scene in a rain forest.
Your friend draws it.

7 Why can't a porcupine smile?

Song.

Sometimes when I'm sitting in the bath,
I think of silly questions which always make me laugh.
Sometimes in the shower or in the bath,
I sing these silly questions which always make me laugh.
And the questions go like this . . .
Why can't a porcupine smile?
Why can't an elephant sing?
Why can't a pelican boil an egg,
When I can do all of these things?
Silly questions make you giggle.
Silly questions make you laugh.
Silly questions don't have answers
When you're in the shower
Or you're sitting in the bath.

Think of some silly questions with your friend.

Remember!
was/were
can/can't
has got
there is/there are

13
thirteen

FACT CARD

What do you know about rain forests?

This is a picture of a tropical rain forest. The weather in the tropics is very hot and wet. The trees in the rain forest grow very tall. There are lots of different kinds of trees. Some trees are seventy metres tall.
The floor of the rain forest is quite dark. There are a lot of dead leaves there, but not many green plants.

4

The leaves at the top of the trees are very thick. They make a canopy. Lots of animals and birds live in the canopy. Smaller plants, like orchids, live on the tree trunks in the canopy. Smaller plants and new trees grow by the side of the rivers. When a tree falls down, new plants can grow in the space.

Once there were a lot of rain forests. Now there aren't many. They are disappearing quickly.

We must look after the rain forests.

1   The rain forests of the world

Listen and point.

Talk about the map with your friend.

Are there any rain forests in the USA?   *No.*

15
fifteen

4

2 Pitcher plants

Listen and look.

Anne

Mark

Susie

Joe

a   b   c   d

Whose plants are they?
Listen and point.

Talk to your friend.

- How tall is Anne's plant?
- Ten centimetres.
- How many leaves has it got?

Draw a plant and talk to your friends about it.

This is my plant.
Its name is Max. Its
favourite food is teachers.

16
sixteen

3 A rain forest quiz

How much can you remember about the rain forest?

1. Are there any rain forests in Africa?
2. What's the weather like in the rain forest?
3. How tall are some trees in the rain forest?
4. Do orchids grow on the floor of the rain forest?
5. What does a pitcher plant eat?

Remember!
How tall …?
How many …?

4 Sunflower in the sun

Song.

Sunflower in the sun, growing very high.
Sunflower in the sun, growing very high.
Sun and water you need to make you grow from a seed.
Till you look like a yellow sun.
Till you look like a yellow sun.

A sunflower grows taller and taller
Till you can't touch its head with your hand.
A sunflower grows bigger and bigger.
It's proud, it's yellow, it's grand.
A giant sunflower is enormous.
It's an incredible height.
I know that sunflowers love the sun,
But what do they do at night?
Please tell me, what do they do at night?

seventeen

5 Find Joseph Alexander

At last they find Joseph Alexander in the Palm House.

> Excuse me, Mr Alexander. We've got a message for you from Professor Wallace.

> At last! This is very important. Please come in. And call me Joe!

Practise with your friends.

1 How shall we go?

Listen and point.

the beach
London
the park
the swimming pool
the safari park
the station

Think of somewhere to go. Talk to your friend.

> Let's go to the swimming pool.
> No, let's go by bike.

> How shall we go? Shall we go by bus?

How can you get to these places?

| the rain forest | Australia | the moon |

nineteen

2 What time does the train leave?

Listen and point.

Departures		Platform
Leeds	9.45	2
London	10.08	5
Bristol	10.30	3
Birmingham	10.50	1
Liverpool	11.18	2
Glasgow	11.27	4

Talk to your friend.

(What time does the train to London leave?) (At eight minutes past ten.)

(Which platform does it leave from?) (Platform 5.)

3 Here in our town

Song.

Here, here in our town, that's the place where I want to be.
Here in our town, here in our town, here in our town!
Because there's a great big church with a marvellous clock,
And a bell that rings when it's twelve o'clock.
Here in our town, there's a beautiful station with electric trains.
Here in our town, there's a nice bus shelter for when it rains.

Because it's the place where I live.
And the place where I eat and have my lunch.
It's the place where I sleep.
Here in our town, it's the place where I play and go to school.
Here in our town, I meet my friends at the swimming pool.

6 London

You can feed the pigeons near Nelson's Column in the middle of Trafalgar Square. There are fountains in the square, too.

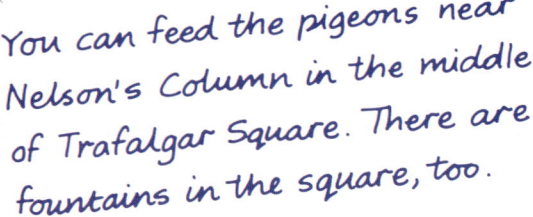

London is the capital of England. The buildings in the picture are the Houses of Parliament. The big clock is called Big Ben. The Houses of Parliament are next to the river Thames.

You can look at the Crown Jewels in the Tower of London, but you can't touch them. The Beefeaters guard the Crown Jewels.

You can visit the Tower of London. It is more than 900 years old.

6

 1   A map of London

Listen and point.

   Talk to your friend about the places on the map.

> Can you find Trafalgar Square?

> Yes, here it is. It's to the north of the Houses of Parliament.

2   What do the signs mean?

Read and match.

> Stop.   Turn right.   Turn left.
>
> Don't go in here.
>
> Don't park your car here.

   Talk to your friend.

> What does this sign mean?

> Turn right.

23

twenty-three

3 Asking for directions

Listen to some directions. Follow them on the map.

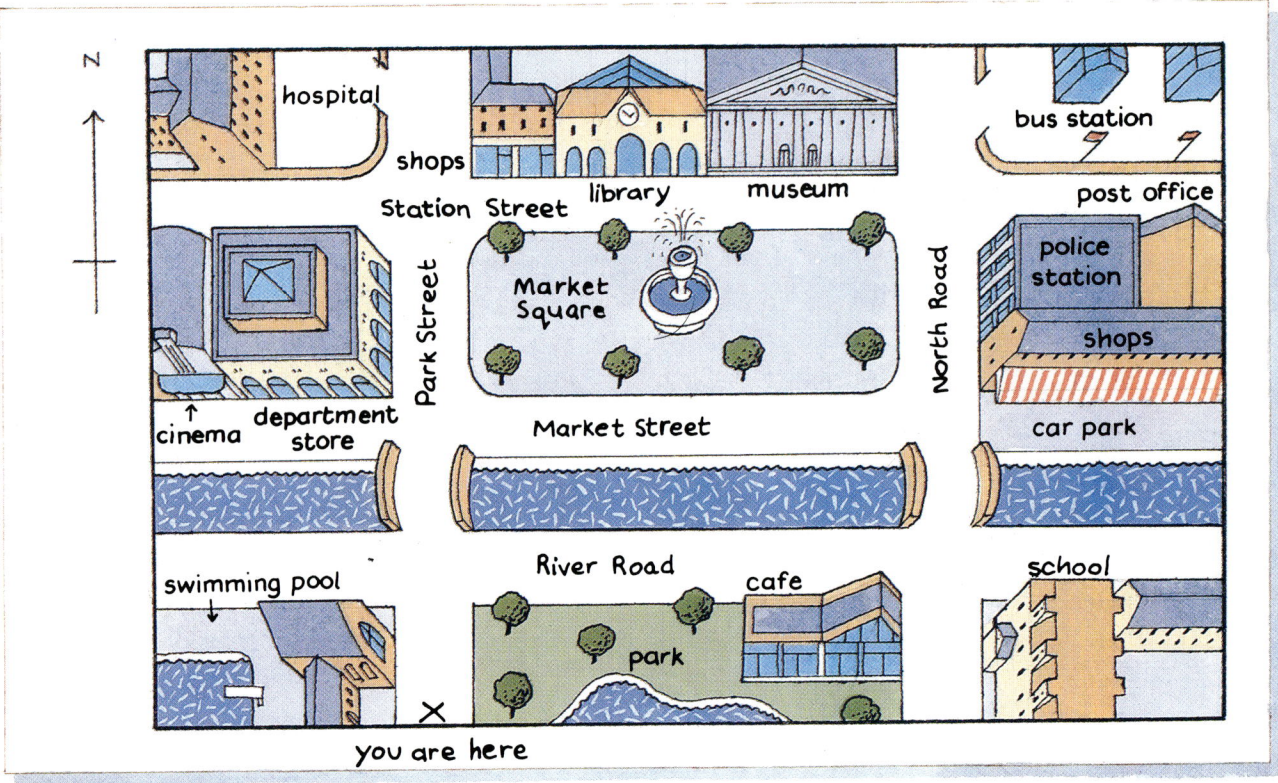

Listen and practise with your friend.

A: Excuse me, can you tell me the way to the police station, please?
B: Yes, of course. Go down Park Street and turn right. Go down River Road. Then turn left. Go down North Road. The police station's on the right.
A: Thank you.
B: That's all right.

How do you get to these places on the map?
Ask for and give directions with your friend.

| the | school   cinema   post office   museum   hospital |

4 Our town

Read the two descriptions of the town on page 24 and say which is the right one.

This is our town. There is a big square called Market Square in the middle of the town. There are some shops and a library on the north side of Market Square and there's a big department store on the west side. The school is to the south of the river, opposite the car park.

This is our town. It has got a bus station and a train station. There's a hospital near the park. The park is south of the hospital. The big square in the middle of the town is called Market Square. The police station is on the east side of the square.

Talk to your friend about the town.

What's in the middle of Market Square?   A fountain.

Where's the car park?   Opposite the department store.

5 Where do you live?

Draw a map and show your friend where you live.

What's the capital city of your country?
What interesting places can you see there?
Can you name an art gallery,
a cathedral, a museum, a square and a river?

Remember!
please/thank you
Excuse me . . .
That's all right.
Go down . . .
Turn left/right.
It's on the left/right.

25
twenty-five

7 Off we go!

Joseph Alexander is going to help Professor Wallace.
Kate and Sam are going to travel with him.

 Practise with your friends.

1 What do they need?

 Look at the equipment and listen to the conversation.
Point to the things they are going to take.

2 What do they need?

 Look at the equipment again. Listen and answer Sam and Kate's questions.

7

3 Hobbies

What are they going to take? Read and match.

This is Tina. She's twelve. Her hobby is skiing. She's going to go skiing in Austria.

This is Paul. He's thirteen. His hobby is making films. He and his friends are going to make a film in Brazil.

This is Kamala. She's eleven. Her hobby is bird-watching. She's going to look for eagles in Canada.

A

B

C

4 What do they need?

Talk to your friend.

- Why does Tina need a pair of skis?
- Because she's going to go skiing in Austria.

5 My holiday

Imagine you are going on holiday. What do you need? Make a list and talk to your friend about it.

- I need a camera.
- Why?
- Because I'm going to take some photos.

6 Whenever you go on a journey

Song.

Whenever you go on a journey
To Morocco or maybe to Spain,
A map shows you where you're going
And a timetable tells you the time,
The time of your train.
So that's why
I'm waiting at the station
With my timetable and my map.
And I'm happy
'Cause I know where I'm going,
And I know when I'm coming back.

Whenever you go on a journey
To Brazil or maybe Bahrain,
A map shows you where you're going,
And a timetable tells you the time,
The time of your plane.
So that's why
I'm waiting at the airport
With my timetable and my map.
And I'm happy
'Cause I know where I'm going,
And I know when I'm coming back.
Yes, I know when I'm coming back.

7 Find the people

Listen and point to the people in the picture.

Talk to your friend about the picture.

Remember!
going to . . .
I need . . .
Why? Because . . .

29
twenty-nine

8 A project about volcanoes

This is an active volcano in Iceland. It is erupting. There are about 500 active volcanoes in the world.

Some volcanoes do not erupt. They are not active, they are extinct.

Can you name an active volcano? Can you name an extinct volcano?

Where are the world's active volcanoes?

This picture shows where the active volcanoes are. Is there one in your country?

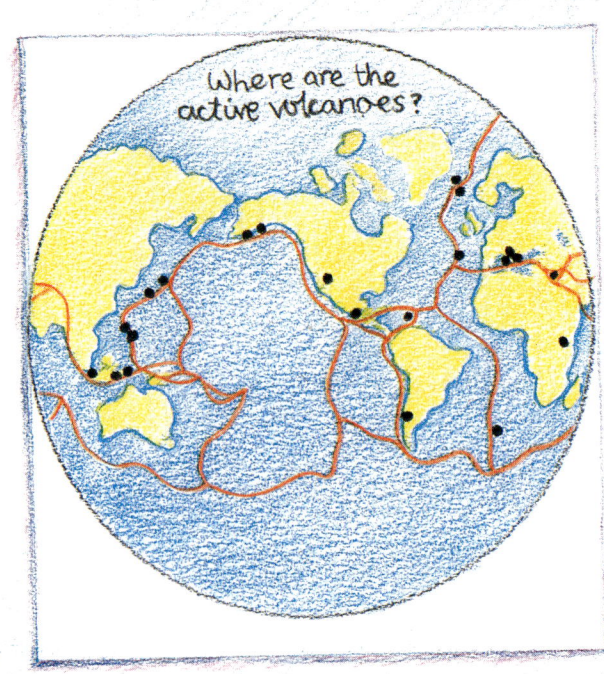

8

It is very hot inside the earth. When rock and metal become very hot they melt. They become liquid.

There are also gases inside the earth. Sometimes these gases escape through a crack in the earth. The gases carry the liquid rock and metal with them. This is what happens when a volcano erupts.

rock   metal   water   ice   steam   oxygen   milk

1   True or false?

Listen and say.

2   Liquids, solids and gases

Listen and point.

Talk to your friend.

> Show me a liquid.

> Here. Water is a liquid.

What other liquids, solids and gases can you name?

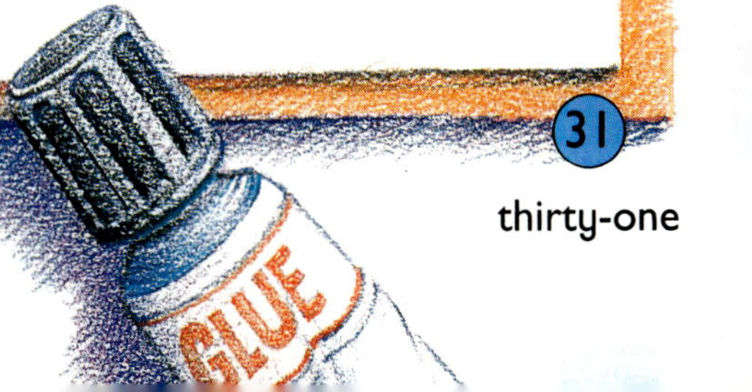

3   Rumble and shake

 Song.

It starts with a slow steady rumble.
It starts with a slow steady shake.
It blows clouds of steam like an engine.
The sleeping volcano awakes.

Then the mountain shakes and rumbles
Throws hot rocks into the sky.
Molten rock and molten metal
Will cause everything to die.

Then the people shake and tremble
As the molten river runs.
St Helens is erupting
And it's like a thousand suns.

Then the molten river hardens
And the steam just drifts away.
But the earth is only sleeping.
It can wake up any day.

4   Which of these things melt when you heat them?

 Listen and say.

| butter | eggs | rock | bread | chocolate | paper | ice |

Talk to your friend.

– Does chocolate melt when you heat it?
– Yes, it does.

Remember!
Water is a liquid.
Ice is a solid.
Steam is a gas.
Chocolate melts when you heat it.

32
thirty-two

8

5 Pompeii

Listen and point.

A street.

Beware of the Dog.

Actors.

Vesuvius 79 AD

A project. Find out about a famous monument in your country. Write about it. Draw pictures and collect photos for your project.

9

They walked to the village. Joe talked to the villagers.

At last they reached the cliffs.

We're looking for Professor Wallace.

She was here about ten days ago. She wanted to go to the Blue Mountains.

Look! The professor! I can see her!

Practise with your friends.

1 Where did they go?

Listen and follow the directions on the map.

2 Tell the story

Listen and repeat.

passed	stopped	
arrived	asked	followed
crashed		walked
crossed	climbed	reached

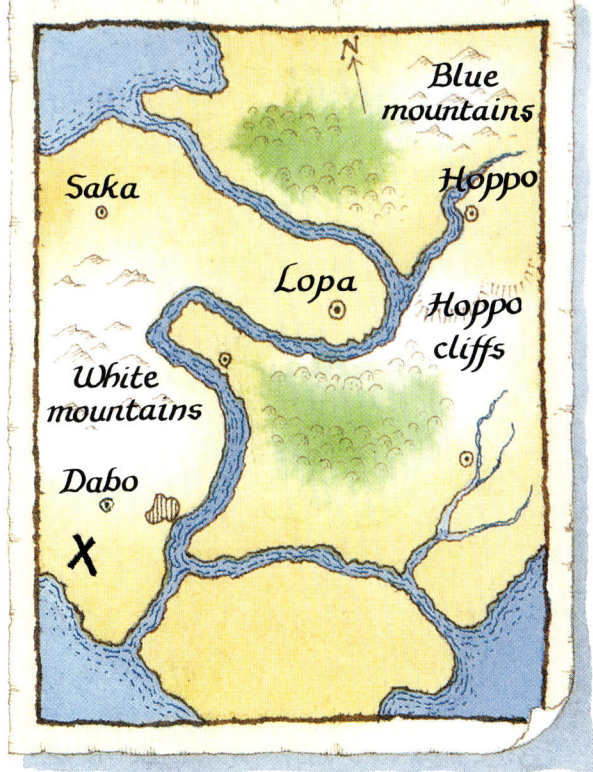

Tell the story with your friend.

First their plane ...   *Then they ...*

35

thirty-five

3   Kate's diary
Read and match.

Monday
The professor mended the rope ladder.

Tuesday
Beano climbed a tree.

Wednesday
Everybody played in a waterfall.

Thursday
Joe cooked an enormous meal.

Friday
I helped the professor to look for orchids.

Saturday
A monkey chased Sam.

4   Who climbed a tree?

Talk to your friend.

(Who climbed a tree on Tuesday?)   (Beano!)

5   A game

Write down an activity and put it in a hat.
Choose one and then ask the class.

(Who played tennis?)   (Maria!)

36
thirty-six

9

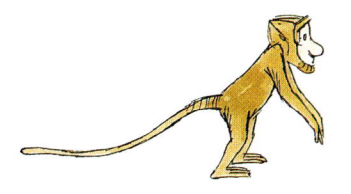

6 Find the treasure

Look at the map and find the missing words.

| was   crossed   climbed   reached   landed   walked   followed |

Our ship ~~~~~~ at Deep Bay. We ~~~~~~ the Snake River to Crater Lake. We ~~~~~~ the lake on a raft. Then we ~~~~~~ through the haunted forest. We ~~~~~~ Redbeard's castle. Some pirates chased us, but we escaped and ~~~~~~ the Icy mountain. The treasure ~~~~~~ in a cave.

Talk about another way to find the treasure.

7 My treasure map

your turn! Draw your own treasure map and talk to your friend about it.

What's this?   It's the Crocodile River!

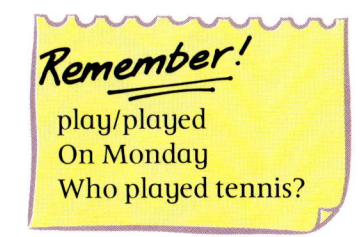

Remember!
play/played
On Monday
Who played tennis?

37
thirty-seven

10 Life in the rain forest

Orangutans come from the forests of southeast Asia. People are looking after these baby orangutans because they haven't got any mothers. When the babies grow up they can go back to their homes in the wild.

This flying squirrel lives in the canopy of the rain forest. It 'flies' from tree to tree.

There are lots of beautiful birds in the rain forest. They are in danger because people sometimes catch them and sell them for pets.

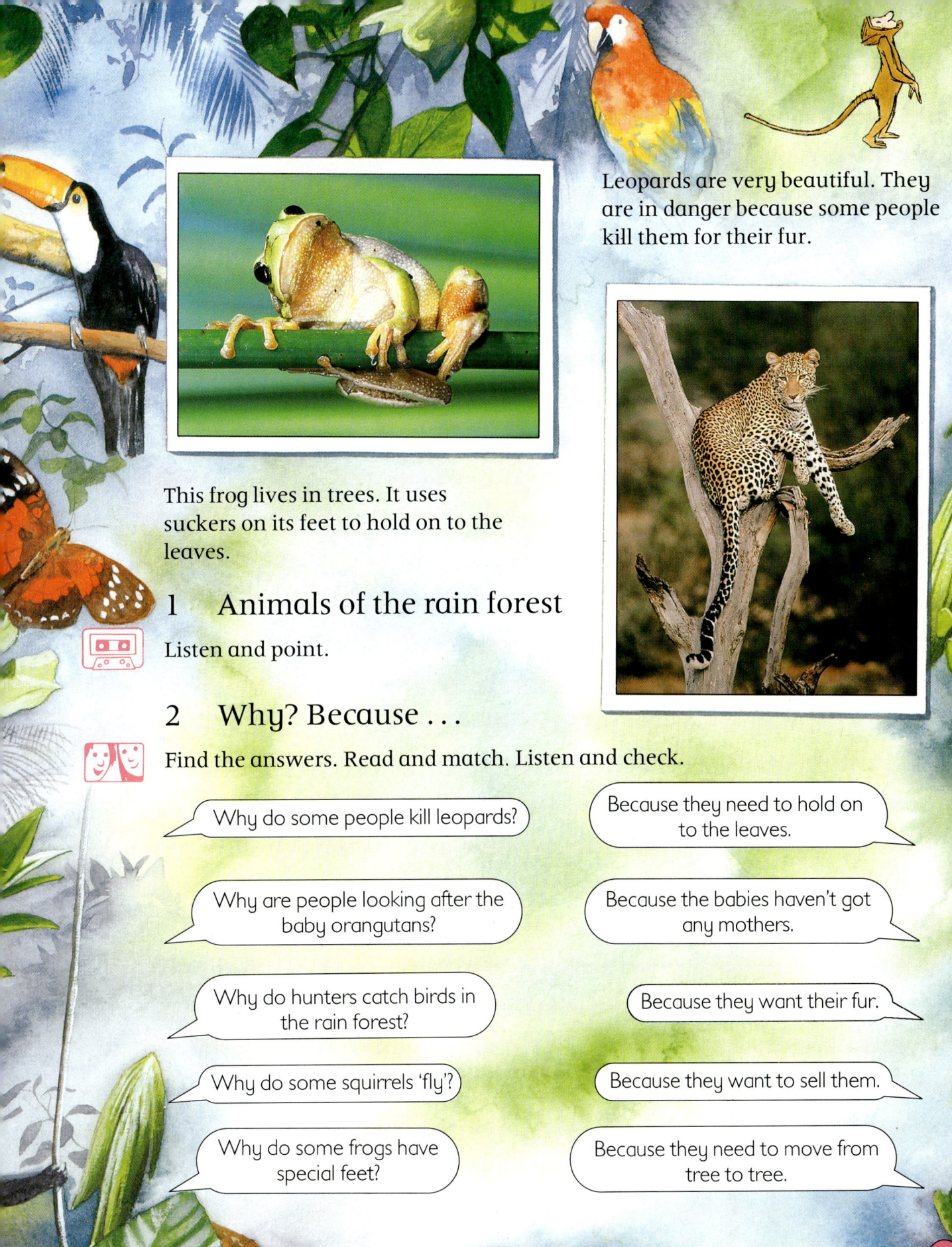

Leopards are very beautiful. They are in danger because some people kill them for their fur.

This frog lives in trees. It uses suckers on its feet to hold on to the leaves.

1   Animals of the rain forest

Listen and point.

2   Why? Because …

Find the answers. Read and match. Listen and check.

- Why do some people kill leopards?
- Why are people looking after the baby orangutans?
- Why do hunters catch birds in the rain forest?
- Why do some squirrels 'fly'?
- Why do some frogs have special feet?

- Because they need to hold on to the leaves.
- Because the babies haven't got any mothers.
- Because they want their fur.
- Because they want to sell them.
- Because they need to move from tree to tree.

39

thirty-nine

3 A garden safari

Read and match.

1 This animal is brown. It's bigger than a squirrel.
2 This bird is smaller than a blackbird. It's brown and red.
3 This bird is black and it's got a yellow beak.
4 This animal is smaller than a badger. It's brown. It's got a long tail. It climbs trees.
5 This animal is bigger than a rabbit. It's grey, black and white.
6 This animal is smaller than a fox. It's brown. It's got long ears. It doesn't like foxes!

4 Garden explorers

Bernard and Tina watched the animals in the park. Listen to their telephone conversation. What did Bernard see? Listen and point to the animals.

Look at Tina's notebook. What did she see? Talk to your friend.

How many badgers did Tina see?

She didn't see any, but she saw a fox.

Act out an interview with Tina or Bernard.

Remember!
How many . . . ?   bigger than . . .
Why?/Because . . .   smaller than . . .

Monday 12th May
squirrels ✓✓✓✓✓✓✓✓
foxes ✓
rabbits ✓✓✓✓✓
robins ✓✓
blackbirds ✓✓✓✓
badgers

11 The Angel of the Forest

There's a lot to learn in the rain forest.

1.
- What's the orchid called?
- The Angel of the Forest.
- Why do you want to find it?
- Because I can make a medicine with it. It can help millions of people all over the world.

But there are dangers, too.

2.
- Never go anywhere without one of us. It's wetter here than in England. There can be flash floods. It's hotter than England, too. There can be volcano action at any time.

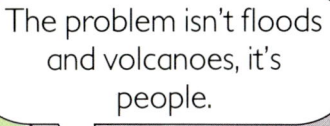

3.
- The problem isn't floods and volcanoes, it's people.
- Why?
- Because somebody cut the professor's rope ladder and somebody stole things from the professor's bag.

4a / 4b.
- What are those idiots doing? Where's my orchid?

Practise with your friends.

41

forty-one

1 The Pink Parrot Gang

Puzzle. Read and find the names of the Pink Parrots.

Pip is taller than Pam and Jem but she isn't taller than Polly. Polly has got shorter hair than Pam. Pam is thinner than Pip. Jem has got longer hair than Pam. Pam has got smaller feet than Polly and Polly has got a bigger nose than Jem.

Talk about the Pink Parrot Gang with your friend.

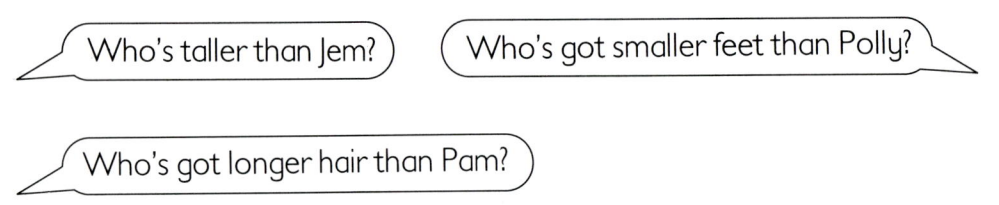

- Who's taller than Jem?
- Who's got smaller feet than Polly?
- Who's got longer hair than Pam?

2 Our class

Measure the people in your class. Talk about their height.

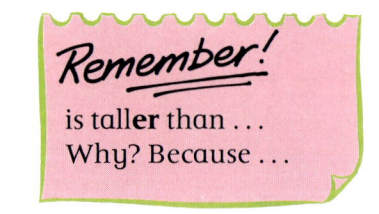

- Is Mark taller than Carla?
- Yes, he is.

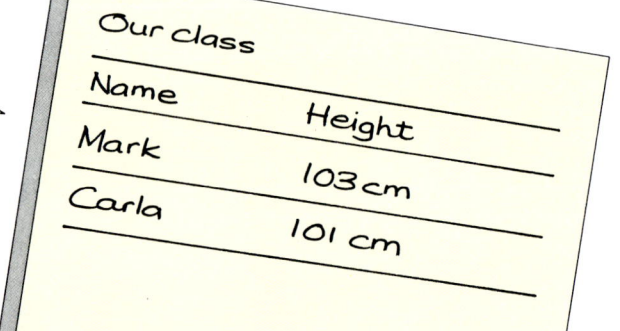

Remember!
is tall**er** than ...
Why? Because ...

Our class

Name	Height
Mark	103 cm
Carla	101 cm

3 Kelvin and Gwen

Look at the photos of Kelvin and Gwen. Where do you think they come from? Then listen to the letter cassettes and point to the correct countries.

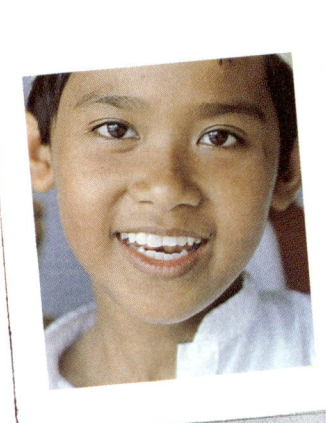

Name: Kelvin Tam
Age: 11 years and 3 months
Height: 1m 28cm
Weight: 36kg
Family: one sister
Dog: Sammy

Name: Gwen Robinson
Age: 11
Height: 1m 30cm
Weight: 35kg
Family: two brothers
Dog: Rollo

Singapore

Size: 620km²
Population: 2,600,000
Weather: Tropical

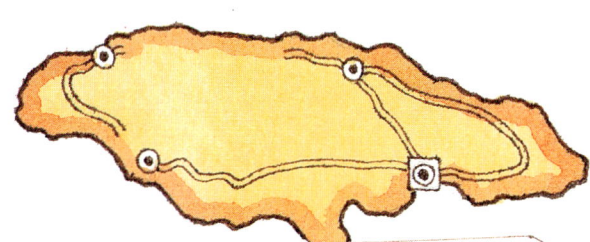

Jamaica

Size: 10,962km²
Population: 2,400,000
Weather: Hot and sunny

Talk about Gwen and Kelvin with your friend.

- Who's older, Gwen or Kelvin?
- Where does Kelvin come from?
- How tall is Gwen?

How are you different from Gwen and Kelvin? Are you older? Are you taller? What is your country like? Talk to your friend.

forty-three

12 A project about water

Everybody needs water. Where does your water come from?

Plants need water to grow. When the rain falls, lots of plants grow. What happens when there is no rain?

This picture shows how rain is made. The sun heats the water in the sea. The water turns into steam and rises. When the steam gets cold, it turns into tiny drops of water which make clouds. When these drops get big and heavy, they turn into rain and fall to the ground.

We need clean water to drink. 70% of our body is made up of water. Each of us needs 2.5 litres of water per day. Animals need water, too.

44
forty-four

12

1 Why isn't rain salty?

An experiment. Read and match.

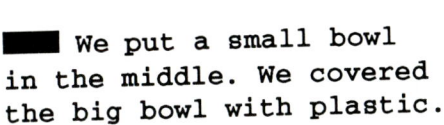

① ④

②

③

▬ We put a small bowl in the middle. We covered the big bowl with plastic.

▬ Water dropped into the small bowl. We tasted the water in the small bowl. It wasn't salty.

▬ We poured boiling water into a bowl. We mixed it with salt.

▬ We put a coin on top of the plastic. We waited for two hours.

2 What did they do?

Answer the questions.

1 How many bowls did they need?
2 Did they pour the boiling water into the small bowl?
3 What did they do with the plastic?
4 Did they wait for one hour?
5 Did the water in the small bowl taste salty?

your turn!

What do you need for this experiment? Talk to your friend.

12

3   What do you do when ...?

Talk to your friends.

> What do you do when you get cold?

> I put on a jumper.

Use these words.

| get | hungry   cold   hot   tired   wet   thirsty |

A joke

WHAT ANIMAL LIKES GETTING WET?
A REINDEER

4   What does it taste/smell/feel like?

Listen and point.

| salty   sweet   sour   hot | soft   wet   cold   slimy | horrible   lovely |

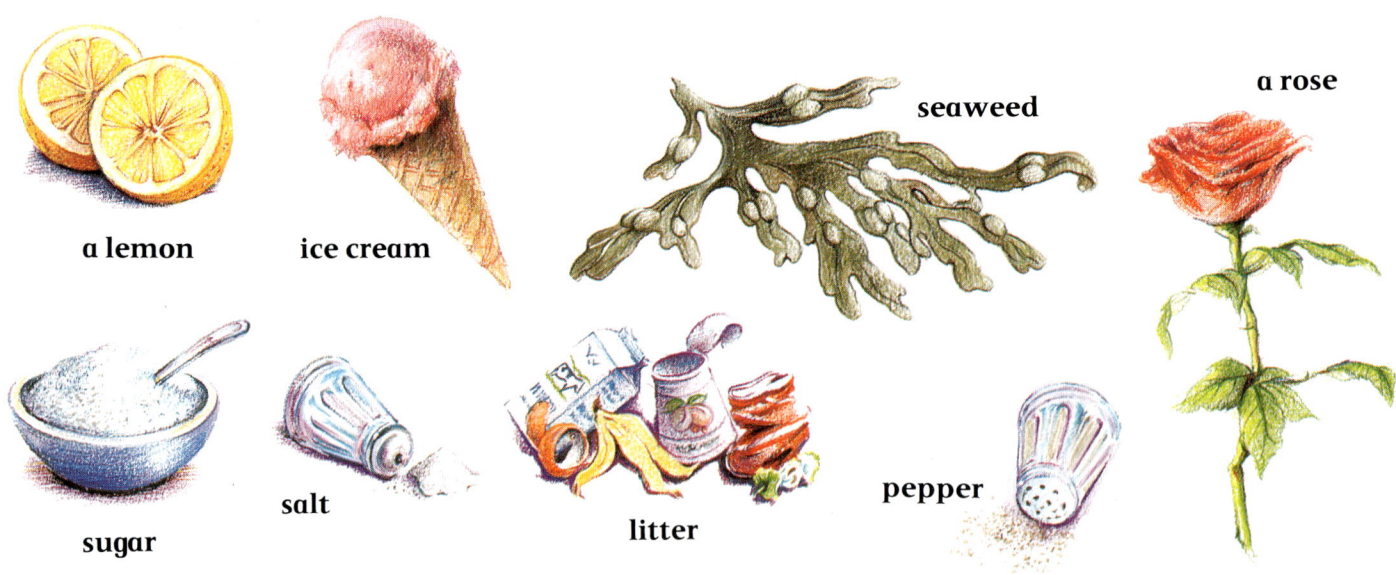

a lemon

ice cream

seaweed

a rose

sugar

salt

litter

pepper

silk

Talk to your friend.

> What does a lemon taste like?

> It tastes sour.

Try your own taste/smell/feel test.

forty-six

12

5 River valley

Game. Can you find the River valley orchids?

1 START

2 Ask for directions. Go to 4.

3

4

5 Wait for the boat. Miss a turn.

6

7 Find a boat. Go down the river to 15.

8

9 Stop to cook some food. Miss a turn.

10

11 Where is your water bottle? Go back to 8.

12

13

14 The bridge is broken. Miss a turn.

15

16 Wrong way! Go back to 4.

17 Follow some people through the forest. Go to 20.

18

19

20 There's a secret path through the waterfall. Go to 27.

21

22 You feel hot and want to swim. Miss a turn.

23

24

25

26 A crocodile! Run to 28.

27

28

29 Eat some strawberries. They taste delicious. Miss a turn.

30 The orchids! Well done!

Remember!

What do you do when . . .
gets (cold)
What does it smell/taste/feel like?
It tastes . . .

13 A shape in the mist

Sam and Kate are helping Professor Wallace to look for the Angel of the Forest. They like exploring the rain forest. They are a long way from their camp.

1. Sam, it's getting late … and now it's going to rain!

Here's a cave. Let's shelter here.

2. I don't like it in here. There's a funny smell and look, there are lots of bats.

Come on, we aren't afraid of bats. Anyway, the sun's shining. Let's go.

3. Hey, Kate. Is this a footprint? Maybe it's a dinosaur's footprint. It's very big.

Don't be silly!

48 forty-eight

13

"Help! It's a dinosaur! Run!"

"No, it isn't. Look. It's an old building. I think it's a pyramid."

"Don't be silly! Pyramids are in Egypt, not Indonesia!"

Practise with your friends.

1 Footprints

Whose footprints are they? Talk to your friend.

dog
cat
fox
frog
bird
elephant
horse

"Whose footprint is this?"

"I think it's a dog's footprint."

Draw a footprint. Whose is it? Ask your friend to guess.

49

forty-nine

13

2 What do they like doing?

Listen and match the names with the photos.

Takahisa

Karl   Elaine   Andreas   Ingrid

1

2

3

4

5

Talk to your friend.

What does Ingrid like?   She likes skiing.

3 Do you like painting pictures?

Ask your friends questions about the things they like doing.

Do you like painting pictures?   No, not really, but I like taking photos.

50
fifty

13

4 Things that go bump in the night

Song.

Just imagine that you're lying there,
Quite terrified with fright,
From those GROANS and CREAKS and NOISES
Those things that go bump in the night!

Ask yourself what does it look like?
That horrible face in the dark?
Is it a Frankenstein monster?
Or is it a man-eating shark?

Ask yourself what does it sound like?
That THING that goes tappity-tap?
Is it a hairy gorilla?
Or is it a blood-sucking bat?

Bumpity-bump, it is coming. It is coming slowly upstairs.
Bumpity-bump, it is coming. Cover your eyes and your ears.
Bumpity-bump, it is coming. That horrible THING in the night
And then that voice in the darkness
'Is everything in there all right?'

5 What are you afraid of?

Talk to your friend.

Are you afraid of the dark?

No, but my brother is.

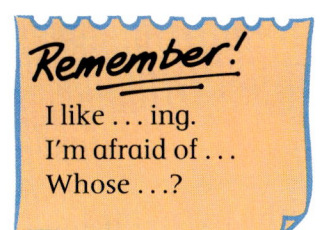

Remember!
I like . . . ing.
I'm afraid of . . .
Whose . . . ?

51
fifty-one

14 Dinosaurs

Dinosaurs lived between 200 million and 65 million years ago. There were many different kinds of dinosaurs. Listen to the description of four dinosaurs and point to the correct pictures.

The stegosaurus

The tyrannosaurus

The triceratops

The iguanodon

14

1 Which dinosaur is it?

Read and match the fact cards to the pictures of the right dinosaur.

A

Length: 12m
Weight: 7000kg
Height: 5m
Food: meat
Special features: claws and long, sharp teeth

B

Length: 6m
Weight: 8500kg
Height: 3m
Food: plants
Special features: three horns on its head

C

Length: 6m
Weight: 2000kg
Height: 3.5m
Food: plants
Special features: plates on its back and spikes on its tail

D

Length: 9m
Weight: 4500kg
Height: 5m
Food: plants
Special features: spikes on its hands

Listen to the descriptions again. Were you right?

2 Test your partner

Pupil A, close your book. Pupil B, ask questions about the dinosaurs.

What did the tyrannosaurus eat?

How tall was it?

How heavy was it?

How long was it?

fifty-three

14

3   Whose bones are they?

Talk to your friend.

I think this is a triceratops.

Why?

Because there are three horns on its head.

4   Find the dinosaurs

Read and match.

the longest dinosaur

the lightest dinosaur

the heaviest dinosaur

the tallest dinosaur

The fiercest dinosaur

the smallest dinosaur

Talk to your friend.

Which dinosaur is the longest?

The tyrannosaurus!

54

fifty-four

14

5. Why did the dinosaurs die?

The dinosaurs lived on earth for more than 100 million years. Then, 65 million years ago, all dinosaurs became extinct. What happened?

1. Some scientists think a giant meteor hit the earth. It made a giant hole in the rock under the sea.

2. Liquid rock erupted from the hole and the sea rushed in. The water turned into steam.

3. A thick cloud of steam and dust covered the whole sky. All over the earth, the weather became very cold.

4. It was too cold for the dinosaurs. They did not have any fur to keep them warm. Many dinosaurs died.

5. The dinosaurs lived in rain forests. The cold weather killed the plants in the forests. So the plant-eating dinosaurs died.

6. When the plant-eating dinosaurs died, the meat-eating dinosaurs had no food. They died, too.

Remember!

long/long**est**   heavy/heav**iest**   ... years ago
Which dinosaur is the biggest?   Whose ...?

fifty-five

15 The painting on the wall

Kate and Sam climbed up to the old building.

"It looks like a temple."

It was dark in the temple. They climbed over some rocks.

There was a picture on the wall.

"Do you think they buried people in here like in the pyramids?"

"I hope not."

"Look, Sam."

"She's beautiful. And look what she's got in her hand!"

"It's the Angel of the Forest!"

15

What's that?

It sounds like a door!

Be quiet, dog!

SLAM!

Oh, no!

Practise with your friends.

1 What does it sound like?

Look at the pictures in the story. Listen and point.

2 Zack's mistakes

Tex and Zack are following Sam and Kate. This is Zack's diary. There are lots of mistakes. Look at the story and find the mistakes.

Correct the mistakes with your friend.

They climbed down to the old building.

No, they didn't. They climbed up to the old building.

It was light inside the temple.

No, it wasn't. It was dark.

MONDAY

They climbed down to the old building. It looked like a school. It was light inside the temple. They climbed over a wall. There was a picture on the ceiling. It was a picture of a boy.

Write some sentences about your friend. Add some mistakes.
Read your sentences to the class. Can they correct the mistakes?

57

fifty-seven

3   A picture gallery

Whose pictures are they? Read and match.

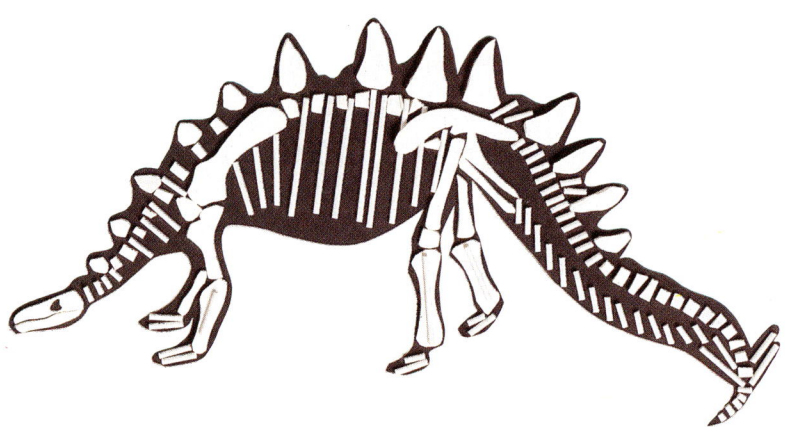

Tony made a collage. He used straws to make a picture of a dinosaur's skeleton.

Sue painted a picture of her father. She used water colours.

Richard made a picture of a garden. He pressed flowers and stuck them on the paper.

Ruth made the other picture. What is it? What did she do?

4   Whose picture is this?

Talk about the pictures with your friend.

- Whose picture is this?
- It's Tony's.
- What is it?
- It's a dinosaur. I think it's a stegosaurus.

15

5 What does it look like?

Play a game with your friend.

39	40 It looks like a volcano.	41	42 It looks like a forest.	43	44	45 Finish
38 They look like birds.	37 It looks like a house.	36	35	34 It looks like a hat.	33	
26	27 It looks like a tree.	28	29	30	31 They look like clouds.	32
25	24 It looks like a bee.	23	22 They look like a dinosaur's bones.	21 It looks like a face.	20	
13 It looks like a spider.	14	15 They look like fish.	16	17 It looks like a cow.	18 It looks like a horse.	19
12 They look like dancers.	11	10 It looks like the sun.	9 They look like apples.	8	7	6 They look like a dinosaur's footprints.
Start	1 It looks like a snail.	2 It looks like a cat.	3	4 It looks like a dog.	5 It looks like a flower.	

Talk to your friend.

> What does this picture look like?

> It looks like a horse.

your turn! Draw some cave paintings. What do they look like? Show them to your friends.

Remember!

What does it sound like/look like?
No, they didn't.
No, it wasn't.
inside/outside
over/under/up/down

59

fifty-nine

16 A real life discovery

EXCITING DISCOVERY IN EGYPT

On 24th February Lord Carnarvon and Mr Howard Carter made an exciting discovery. They found the tomb of Tutankhamun in the Valley of the Kings in Egypt. The magnificent tomb is more than 3000 years old.

When they opened the tomb they found Tutankhamun's clothes, jewellery, furniture and his coffins. The coffins were made of gold.
Daily News, 1922.

These are some of the things from Tutankhamun's tomb. His people put food, clothes, furniture and jewellery there for the young king to use in his next life.

16

Who was Tutankhamun? He was born in Egypt more than 3000 years ago. When he was seven, he got married. His wife's name was Ankhesenamun. Tutankhamun became king of Egypt when he was only nine years old. He was king for nine years, but then he died.

The things that Lord Carnarvon and Howard Carter found in the tomb tell us about the way the young king lived. This is Tutankhamun's mask. It is made of gold.

1 What are they made of?

Listen and point.

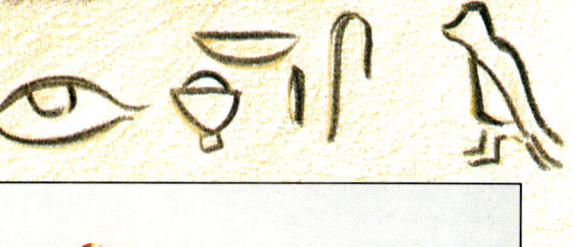

paper
wood
plastic
metal
cotton
glass
rubber

Talk to your friend.

What's this?   It's a mask.   What's it made of?   It's made of plastic.

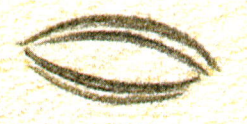

sixty-one

2 The missing mummy

What happened in the museum? Look at the pictures.
Tell the story with your friend.

Read Detective Casey's notes and put them in the correct order.

Talk to your friend.

- What time did the two robbers visit the museum?
- At half past four.

Detective Casey's notes:

- One of the robbers asked the attendant some questions. The other robber hid under the table.
- The robber unlocked a window. Her friends climbed into the museum.
- Detective Casey arrived.
- someone saw a light in the museum and phoned the police.
- The museum closed. The attendant locked all the doors and windows.
- Two robbers visited the museum.

Look at picture 6. Listen and answer the questions.

sixty-two

16

3 How to make a mummy!

How did the Ancient Egyptians make a mummy? Read and match.

First they removed some parts from inside the body. Then they dried the body in a jar for seventy days. After that, they washed the body and wrapped it in bandages to make a mummy. Finally, they put the mummy in a coffin.

Talk about the pictures with your friend.

What did they do first?

They removed ...

4 A picture alphabet

This is Tutenkhamun's name in hieroglyphs.
You can make your own picture alphabet.
Write a sentence in pictures.
Can your friend read it?

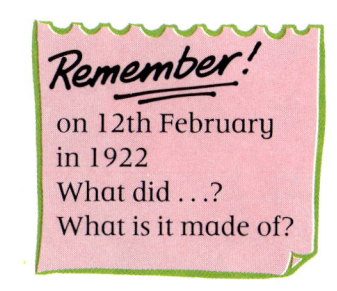

| a | b | c | d | e | f |
| g | h | i | j | k | l |

Remember!
on 12th February in 1922
What did . . .?
What is it made of?

sixty-three

17 The message in the temple

1. What's the matter, Beano? Where are Sam and Kate? Will you show me?

2. Do you think they'll find us, Sam?
Of course they will. Look, that light is coming from somewhere. I've got an idea.

3. Look! Smoke signals.

4. Here you are! I saw your signals.
Look professor, there are lots of pictures.
I've got my camera. We can take some photos.

64 sixty-four

17

"In this one she's picking the orchid."

"Yes, and can you see that rock? It looks like an eagle."

"She's giving the orchid to the young prince. He's ill."

"He'll get better now."

"What shall we do now?"

"Let's look for Eagle Rock and then we'll find the Angel of the Forest."

"Where's Joe?"

Practise with your friends.

1 What's the matter?

Listen and say.

a headache
earache
a stomachache
toothache
a cold
a cough

Everybody is ill. Look at the pictures. Talk to your friend.

"What's the matter with Kate?"

"She's got a headache."

17

2   What will the robbers do?

Listen and follow.

"The robbers are in the white house."

Tell the story with your friend.

"What will the robbers do first?"   "They'll come ..."

3   What will happen in the story?

Look at the story on pages 64 and 65 again.
What do you think will happen next?
Talk to your friend.

"I think Zack will find the Angel of the Forest."

"I don't. I think Joe will find it."

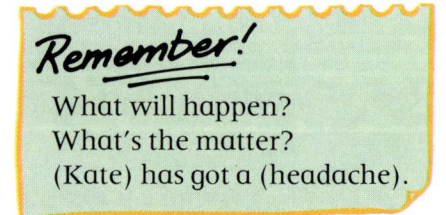

Remember!
What will happen?
What's the matter?
(Kate) has got a (headache).

17

4 The world of the future

What will the world of the future be like?
Read and match.

a

b

c

d

People will build wind farms with lots of windmills.
They will use the wind to make electricity.

Scientists will find plants which will help them to make new medicines.

People won't throw all their rubbish away. They will find ways to use things again.

People will look after the oceans. Animals like dolphins will be safe and healthy.

What do you think will happen?
Make a list with your friend. Show the class.

18 Indonesia

Indonesia has a population of 190 million people. They live on more than 13,000 tropical islands.

Jakarta is the capital of Indonesia. It is a very large modern city on the island of Java.

Many Indonesians live in the countryside. They are farmers. These rice fields are on the island of Bali.

18

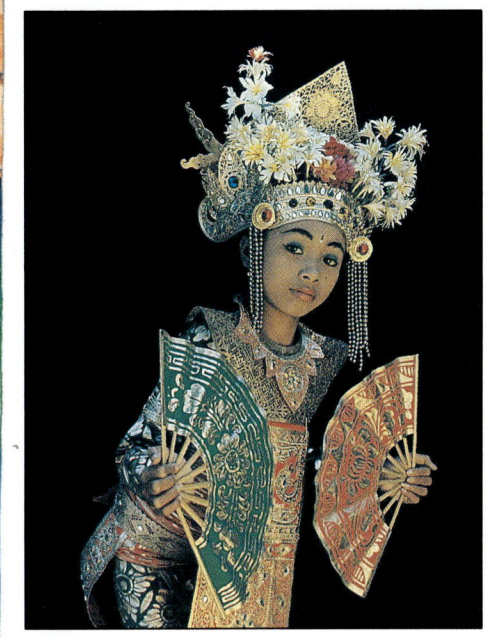

This girl is a dancer from Bali. She is performing the *Legong* dance.

The Komodo dragon lives on the island of Komodo, where the weather is hot and dry. It is the biggest reptile in the world – three metres long. Komodo dragons are very dangerous.

1 A journey to Indonesia

Listen to Scott and Tina.
They are talking about their holiday in Indonesia.
Where did they go? What did they see? Listen and point.

Talk to your friend.

Did they go to Jakarta?

Yes.

What did they see there?

They saw …

What did they buy?

sixty-nine

2 How do you make a shadow puppet?

Look at the pictures and read.

1. You need — thin straight sticks, thin card, paper fasteners, needle and thread
2. Cut out the puppet. 
3. Join the arms with paper fasteners. 
4. Sew on sticks. 
5. Shine a light on a sheet.

Make a puppet with your friend.
Pupil A, close your book. Pupil B, give instructions.

3 Souvenirs

What souvenirs can you buy from your country? Where do they come from? What are they made of?

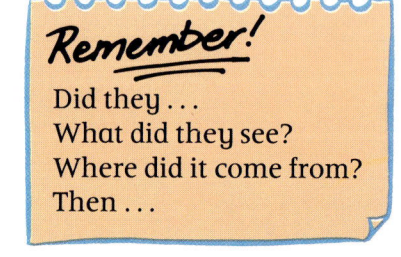

Remember!
Did they . . .
What did they see?
Where did it come from?
Then . . .

18

4 Race track!

Game.

START

1, 2

3 Are your feet bigger than your friend's?

4, 5, 6

7 Is your hair shorter than your friend's?

8, 9

10 Is your house nearer the school than your friend's?

11, 12

13 Is your hair longer than your friend's?

14, 15

16 Are you taller than your friend?

17, 18, 19

20 Are your feet smaller than your friend's?

21, 22

23 Are you younger than your friend?

24, 25, 26

27 Are you older than your friend?

28 Are you shorter than your friend?

29 Is your house further from the school than your friend's?

30. Is your voice louder than your friend's?

31 Is your voice softer than your friend's?

32, 33

FINISH

YES Go forward 2 squares
NO   Go back 2 squares

19 Where is Mr Big?

Zack and Tex searched the campsite. But Joe arrived with the police. The police took Zack and Tex away. Joe went to find his friends.

"Hurry up!"

"Here they are! Let's get out of here!"

"Not so fast, Zack!"

"Arrest those men!"

"It's Joe! Look Joe! We found the Angel of the Forest!"

"Look Joe! This is where the orchid grows."

19

"And these friends of mine are going to look after the orchids. Nobody can steal them now!"

"What's Beano doing?"

Practise with your friends.

1 What will happen next?

Listen and point.

Talk to your friend.

2 Litter in the park

Where did the park keeper find these things? Listen and point.

cola can   crisp packet   ticket   orange peel   comic

Who dropped the litter? Read and match.

Claire
Yes, I was in the park, but I didn't eat or drink anything. I just sat quietly and read something.

James
I didn't go into the park after school. I went home by bus. I ate some fruit at the bus stop.

Matthew
I walked across the park, then I saw my friends playing football. I didn't have anything to eat, but I was thirsty after school.

Fiona
I sat on a bench with my friend and we watched the ducks on the lake. Yes, I had something to eat. I'm always hungry after school.

19

3 The dolphin song

Remember the beautiful dolphins,
And the creatures that live in the seas.
Don't spoil the world you live in.
Remember the dolphins, please!
Remember the dolphins, please!

Oh, you shouldn't throw stones at birds,
And you shouldn't break down a tree.
And you shouldn't throw plastic bottles
Out in the middle of the sea,
Out in the middle of the sea.

My name is King Dolphin,
And I rule all the seas,
Make the world a better place.
Remember the dolphins, please!
Remember the dolphins, please!

4 A predictions game.

Write some predictions. Put them into a hat.
Choose one. Talk to your friend.

What will happen to me?

You'll be a famous scientist.

Remember!
What will happen next?
I didn't . . .

20 Going home

At last, Kate and Sam arrived home. Their families met them at the airport.

"Welcome home, both of you!"

Welcome home Sam and Kate

The local radio interviewed Sam...

"And then we flew over the rain forest..."

"Did you find Mr Big?"

... and Kate appeared on television.

"Where is Mr Big?"

"We don't know. He lives on an island."

They visited Beano in quarantine.

"Never mind, Beano. You'll be home in six months' time!"

Then they went back to school.

"And now Kate and Sam are going to tell us about their trip."

Practise with your friends.

20

1 Which is Mr Big's island?

Read and find.

This is all we know about Mr Big's island.

1. It's one of the islands in this group.
2. It isn't the largest island in the group.
3. It isn't the smallest island in the group.
4. There aren't any other islands near his island.
5. There are a lot of islands to the north of his island.
6. There's only one island to the east of it.

2 Kate's interview

Listen and find her answers.

At Kew Gardens.

At a place called Eagle Rock.

No, we didn't see him.

On Sam's computer.

Three – Zack, Tex and Polly Zap.

Yes, it was very exciting!

your turn! Now listen and repeat the interviewer's questions.
Interview Sam and Kate.

seventy-seven

20

3 Medicine from the forest

The rosy periwinkle

This little plant from the rain forest saves thousands of lives every year. In the 1960s scientists discovered that they could use it to make a medicine that cures some kinds of cancer.

How do people get medicine from the forests? Read and match.

A

B

C

D

E

People who live in the rain forests collect plants. They use the plants in many different ways. Sometimes they make medicines from the plants. When scientists go to the forests they ask about the plants that grow there. Then scientists can study the plants in laboratories and learn how to make medicines from them. Then factories make lots of the new medicine to give to people who are ill.

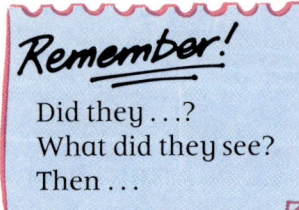

Remember!
Did they . . . ?
What did they see?
Then . . .

78

seventy-eight

20

4   Children of the sun

Song.

We are the children of the sun
And we're telling everyone
That many creatures are in danger now.
As men destroy the world
Then every boy and girl
Must help to show the other people how.

Yes we must fight to save the tiger and the kangaroo.
Yes we must fight to save the panda and the leopard, too.
We'll save the eagle and the whale.
We know we cannot fail.
So join hands all you children of the sun.

We are the children of the sun
And we're telling everyone
That many forests are in danger now.
As men destroy the world
Then every boy and girl
Must help to show the older people how.

What can you do to save the world?
Make a poster with your friends.

Longman Group UK Limited,
Longman House, Burnt Mill, Harlow, Essex CM20 2JE, England and Associated Companies throughout the world.

© Longman Group UK Limited 1994

All rights reserved; no part of this publication may be reproduced, stored in a retrieval system, or transmitted in any form or by any means, electronic, mechanical, photocopying, recording, or otherwise, without the prior written permission of the Publishers.

First published 1994
ISBN 0 582 09918 8

Designed by Anne Samuel
Illustrated by Gary Andrews, Kathy Baxendale, David Cockburn, Neil Gower, Rod Holt, Malcolm Livingstone, Steve Noon, Clive Pritchard (Wildlife Art Agency), Lisa Scott, Martin Shovel, Steve Smallman (B. L. Kearley Ltd), Taurus Graphics, Andy Wagner, Nicola Witt

Music by John Du Prez
Music for 'Rumble and Shake' by Vince Cross
Song Lyrics by Brian Abbs and Anne Worrall

Set in 13/14½ pt. Meridien and 13/16 pt. Gill Sans

Printed in Spain
by Gráficas Estella

British Library Cataloguing-in-Publication Data.
A catalogue record for this book is available from the British Library.

We are grateful to the following for permission to reproduce copyright photographs:

Ancient Art & Architecture Collection for page 33 (top right); Britstock- IFA Ltd for pages 6 (top right), 22 (top left), 38 (bottom), 50 (top left) and 68 (right); Bruce Coleman Ltd for pages 16 and 38 (top left); Colorific!/John Drysdale for page 22 (bottom right); Lupe Cunha for page 28 (right); Greg Evans Photolibrary for page 43 (right); Eye Ubiquitous for page 44 (left); The Griffith Institute, Ashmolean Museum, Oxford for page 60 (top); Robert Harding Picture Library for pages 7 (top), 33 (bottom), 60 (bottom & middle right) and 61 (top); Reproduced with permission of the controller of Her Majesty's Stationery Office for page 23; The Image Bank/Michael Chua for page 43 (left); Frank Lane Picture Agency for page 30; Longman Photographic Unit for pages 27, 58 and 61 (bottom); George Fischer/Bilderberg/Network Photographers for page 7 (bottom) and Barry Lewis/Network Photographers for page 50 (top left); Oxford Scientific Films Ltd for pages 38 (top right) and 69 (right); Photographers Library for page 50 (middle left); Pictor International Ltd for pages 44 (right), 50 (middle right) and 68 (left); By permission of The Trustees, The Royal Botanic Gardens, Kew for page 20; Science Photolibrary for page 6 (bottom right); Tony Stone Worldwide Photolibrary for pages 4, 6 (top left), 14, 22 (top right), 33 (top left), 67 (top right, middle left & middle right) and 69 (left); Telegraph Colour Library for pages 22 (bottom left) and 39 (right); Zefa Picture Library (UK) Ltd for pages 6 (bottom left), 28 (left & middle), 39 (left), 50 (middle) and 67 (top left).

Picture Research by Ann Hazelwood.